1994

AMERICAN MARKETING ASSOCIATION

MARKETING

TOOLBOX

Selecting the Right Products and Services

David Parmerlee

NTC Business Books

a division of *NTC Publishing Group* • Lincolnwood, Illinois USA

This book is dedicated to every young child
with learning disabilities.

Library of Congress Cataloging-in-Publication Data

Parmerlee, David.
    AMA marketing toolbox. Selecting the right products and services / David Parmerlee.
      p. cm.
    Includes index.
    1. Marketing—Management—Data processing. 2. Product management—Data processing I. Title.
    HF5415.125.P35 1992
    658.8'00285—dc20
                                                            92-14250
                                                              CIP

Published in conjunction with the American Marketing Association
250 South Wacker Drive, Chicago, Illinois, 60606.
Published by NTC Business Books, a division of NTC Publishing Group
4255 West Touhy Avenue, Lincolnwood (Chicago), Illinois 60646-1975, U.S.A.
2 3 4 5 6 7 8 9 0 VP 9 8 7 6 5 4 3 2 1

AMA Marketing Toolbox

Many marketing management books define marketing and provide terminology definitions. The *AMA Marketing Toolbox* has a different purpose. This series will guide you in collecting, analyzing, and articulating marketing data. Although there is some narrative that describes the components of marketing processes, these books define the relationships between the processes and explain how they all work together. The books also supply formats (or templates) to help you create sophisticated marketing documents from your data.

A SYSTEMATIC PROCESS . . .
Because markets change constantly and new marketing techniques appear all the time, a step-by-step system is needed to ensure accuracy. These books are process-based to allow you to be as thorough as possible in your marketing activities and document preparation.

. . . FOR PROFESSIONALS
Although these books are written with a "how-to" theme, they are written for marketers who have experience and who know marketing terminology and the objectives of the business function of marketing. The *AMA Marketing Toolbox* consists of the following books:

- *Identifying the Right Markets*

- *Selecting the Right Products and Services*

- *Evaluating Marketing Strengths and Weaknesses*

- *Developing Successful Marketing Strategies*

- *Preparing the Marketing Plan*

ROLE OF THE PRODUCT ANALYSIS

How does the product analysis you will perform in these books fit in with other market planning processes? The product analysis tells a story about a product and explains how to identify and manage it. The analysis tells you about the product's sales performance and its profitability. A product analysis can be tailored to any size company with any product or service.

The books in the *AMA Marketing Toolbox* series will help you go from data collection, to analysis, to planning and control, and eventually to implementation of marketing plans. The diagram below indicates where the books fit into this process.

Data Collection
Research

Primary

Secondary

Database

Internal Audit

Analysis and Planning

Identifying the Right Markets

Selecting the Right Products and Services

Evaluating Marketing Strengths and Weaknesses

Control

Developing Successful Marketing Strategies

Preparing the Marketing Plan

Implementation

Contents

Introduction

WHAT IS A PRODUCT ANALYSIS?

A product analysis is an attempt at defining, identifying, and then evaluating the structure of a particular thing you sell to generate income. Its function is to apply research data and information that have been collected and tabulated, analyze them, and place them in document form to give a detailed, accurate, and unbiased meaning of your product's value to your company.

The product analysis gives you a clearer understanding in a set format of your product line dynamics. It includes establishing why your products exist and how they can have an impact on the marketplace. A product analysis has to answer the following questions:

What needs do your products meet or what problems do they solve?
How profitable are your products; which are strong or weak?
How many products can you produce now and in the future?
What possible legal actions do you face when marketing your products?
What new products are you or should you be introducing?

WHY PERFORM A PRODUCT ANALYSIS?

The purpose of a product analysis is to identify and define your product offerings today and in the future. This builds a foundation for understanding the elements that affect your products. The key goal in performing the product analysis is to be as objective as possible to "read" your products' value or purpose as it actually is with little or no interpretation.

The analysis should mention the markets targeted with these products or services only as reference points; to do otherwise could result in conclusions slanted toward your product or business, thus giving you an inaccurate picture of your product's well-being and defeating the purpose of the exercise. You are performing product research, and although there is some overlap, this is different than performing market research.

Think of a product analysis as a player evaluation used to select a team to compete in a sporting event. Like a baseball manager, you have certain capabilities—your product offerings—that you believe will allow you to compete and win where the game is played—in the marketplace.

The chicken or the egg question—which comes first—always applies when you are determining market impact versus product impact. In this example, we are assuming that you have already defined and identified your market by performing a market analysis. The environment where you want to compete exists; you are now trying to determine how to select and use the players, your products. To do this, you must assess each product, as well as all your products collectively, to determine their strengths and weaknesses.

The first thing you must do is evaluate your product capabilities—their features and benefits. Then you need to determine where they are in their life cycles; how many good years do they have left? Concurrently, you need to examine each product's contribution to the "team's" efforts. Some contribute more than others; this can be good or bad depending on the individual product's role.

Next, you need to evaluate each product's past and future sales performance. If you have a "rookie player"—a new product—then based on current conditions, you must predict its level of performance. As you perform this exercise, you need to try to identify any "slump," sales fluctuations, to establish patterns. Then you must establish how profitable your products are. With each product, you have made an investment and like any financial risk, you are spending money in the hope of making more money.

Then you need to determine what each product's production capacity is. You also need to find out what the "team's" ability is and what its resources are. Next, you need to determine what your liability is for each product.

Finally, you need to determine what new products will be coming on board through product acquisition and what products you have in the pipeline of research and development activities. How will new products help your product-line team?

Like a pro baseball team, your product line is the way you win, through sales volume and revenues. To win the game you must identify and cultivate "players" who can perform consistently and produce a solid return for your investment.

HOW DOES THE PRODUCT ANALYSIS RELATE TO OTHER MARKETING PLANNING PROCESSES?

There are three components to marketing management: the market, the product, and marketing—the action that gets the product to the market. The product analysis tells a story about your product offerings and explains what, why, how, when, and where your products perform. It tells you if the products you currently have in place will achieve the sales and revenue goals you need to exist in the market. A product analysis should be performed every three to five years. If your market experiences great change every year (e.g., a high-tech market), an annual product analysis may be needed.

The first part of the product analysis is evaluating your products on their own merit, without considering the market. The second part of the product analysis deals with determining which products you should be offering. Here the market has tremendous bearing. At this point, the market drives your product base. You can have the greatest products in the world, but if the market does not want them, your products are unfortunately worthless.

> **The author suggests strongly that you perform the market analysis first, then the product analysis. Understanding of the marketplace structure is needed to judge your products' standing.**

If you are established and desire a product and service profile, it is suggested that you perform a marketing audit. A marketing audit is an instrument used in the data collection of researching an organization's marketing management. The audit allows you to uncover the strengths and weaknesses of managing marketing activities. If yours is a new business, a marketing audit would not be appropriate; a business plan would be a possible alternative. A business plan contains three basic marketing segments: a marketing plan, a product analysis, and a market analysis.

WHAT IF YOU ARE PREPARING A SEPARATE MARKET ANALYSIS?

The product analysis, as stated earlier, is usually part of an overall marketing plan. However, if you are preparing a product analysis as an independent document, it should include the following elements:

1. Title page or cover page

2. Table of contents

3. Executive summary (including the purpose of the analysis and its major findings)

4. Methodology

5. Limitations

6. Product analysis (body of report)

7. Exhibits

HOW SHOULD THIS BOOK BE USED?

This book provides you with a set of product analysis formats to help you prepare a document in which marketing research data can be presented in an organized fashion. Part 1 explains and demonstrates the use of the formats; Part 2 includes the blank formats themselves. Remember, you'll need to conduct product research to perform this analysis. As a result, you should first read through the book to see what types of research you will need.

Modifying the Formats

The processes and formats in this book are designed for a consumer market. They can be adapted to your market's needs, problems, and opportunities. Also, although inherent differences exist between a tangible product and an intangible service, in marketing terms they are the same, and these formats can be used for both. (When addressing service as a support function such as repair and maintenance, however, service becomes a value-added component and is separate from the product or service component.)

Throughout this book, you will be alerted to many possible adjustments you may need to make in the product analysis. To conserve space, each format shows a limited number of lines for products, whereas your firm may have fewer or many more products to consider.

Part 1

Data Analysis

The seven units in this book are designed to lead you through a step-by-step process of organizing data about your products, your sales, your production operation, and your research and development activities in order to create a product analysis document. Before using the formats in this book, you will need to have collected, processed, and tabulated data relevant to your particular products or services. The formats in the book will help you use that data to create a clear, understandable document to direct and shape your marketing efforts.

Each unit measures factors that have an impact on your product line. When needed, the formats evaluate the past three years and the next three years in order to assess trends. The goal is to give you insight on how your products have evolved and the future of your product line. By following the step-by-step process in these seven units, you will have a clear picture of your product line, your production capabilities, your legal situation, and your products under development—all substantiated with hard data in a document that will give you confidence as a marketing decision maker.

Unit 1

Identifying Your Products

The first thing you must do is establish what your current product offerings are. You do this by determining why your products exist, whom they are designed for (the market), and what their value is in terms of features and benefits.

DEFINING YOUR PRODUCT LINE

In defining your product line, you need to establish what your products offer the marketplace and whether they are better than other currently available products. Are your products really meeting the needs of customers, or do they exist because your research and development department likes them? Product purpose and level of customer satisfaction should be determined for both past and present products.

Why Do Your Products Exist?

You need to establish your products' purposes and uses for the target market they address. You need to demonstrate the distinctive factors that make your products better or more valuable.

This includes evaluating past products that have been discontinued to determine why they failed or their value was exhausted. You also evaluate what current products you are offering and what their expected actions are.

The first step in defining your products is establishing what products (by product/production line) you are offering and establishing why you are offering these products by defining what each product does. The format shown at the top of Page 3 provides you a method of viewing each product in your line and then describing each product's purpose or use.

Identifying the Target Market

Every product needs to meet a market. This exercise identifies the specific markets your products are targeted for. Your objective is to assign every product you are marketing to a market.

Each market is structured by elements such as competition and industry standards. (For more information, use the market analysis book in this

---

Format 1

Product Purpose

Past Products (Have been discontinued over the last three years. Ranked by order of product/market introduction date.)

Product	Purpose
Model XY3	*Works on removing stains from clothing*
Model XY2	*Works on clothing to protect from stains*

Present Products (Existing products for sale for the next three years. Ranked by order of product/market introduction date.)

Product	Purpose

---

series.) Yet the driving element in any market is the customer. As result, your description of your target market will be customer-profile based.

When you are defining your customer, keep in mind you can have several customer profiles for each product. You also may have a customer who acts as the buyer, but the end user may be someone totally different (i.e., a parent buys for a child). Use format 2 on Page 4 to identify your target market(s) based on customer profiles. Because of space limitations, these sample descriptions are a little broad. You may need to be more specific by using age, income level, etc. to define your customer.

The final part of defining your products is establishing the distinctive factors that make your product better than the alternatives. Very few products can just exist—they must meet a specific need. Even those products that make claims of being multi-purpose still are offering something they believe to be unique.

Format 2

Target Markets

Past Products (Have been discontinued over the last three years. Ranked by order of product/market introduction date.)

Product	Customer/Target Market(s)
Model XY3	*Women who work and run a household in the U.S.*
Model XY2	*Women and men who don't have time to spend cleaning a house in the U.S.*

Present Products (Existing products for sale for the next three years. Ranked by order of product/market introduction date.)

Product	Customer/Target Market(s)

Use the following format to define your products by the distinctiveness of the product offerings.

Format 3

Distinctive Product Factors

Past Products (Have been discontinued over the last three years. Ranked in order of importance.)

Product	Distinctive Factors
Model ABC	*Worked in seconds—failed because of price.*
Model ABC2	*No mess of other liquids needed. Failed because of competition.*

Present Products (Existing products for sale for the next three years. Ranked in order of importance.)

Product	Distinctive Factors

PROFILING YOUR PRODUCTS

You need to outline your products' features and corresponding benefits in order to establish why they are and will be successful. Attaching distinctive factors to your products will help you determine and define their value. When you are developing these attributes, keep in mind the target market. Make sure you are satisfying the customers' needs or solving their problems.

Features

A feature is an attribute that represents a product's ability to perform the task for which it was designed. In establishing your product's features, you may find it valuable to break down your features into primary and secondary classification. For example, if you are marketing electronic items such as videotape players for the home, you may have hundreds of features. What counts are the features that customers want when making a purchasing decision such as remote control or advanced programming. These would be your primary features.

Benefits

Each feature a product possesses should have a corresponding benefit. A benefit is the value a customer places on a function and/or feeling the product produces through its features. You'll need to cite your product research data to determine how customers view the specific benefits of your product. Just as with features, benefits can be classified into primary and secondary levels of importance. As a result, you'll need to determine which benefits are more important to a customer. This information will be key in later product marketing planning activities such as branding and packaging.

Use the following format to tally your product(s) features and benefits.

Format 4

Product Features and Benefits

Product	Features	Benefits
Model XYZ	All controls are placed on one remote control	Easy to use
Model XY2	Two-step programming system	User-friendly when selecting programs

PROFILING BRAND IDENTITY

In a consumer market, a product's features and benefits are not enough; the product's brand identity is crucial. Depending on the product, the appeal many times is not only what the product can do, but what it looks like. Determining how effective your product's branding has been can be defined in two ways: image and appearance. Image deals with the message the actual product is conveying, and appearance deals with how the product is contained for sale.

Product Image

Many elements drive a customer to make a purchase. You must establish what image your product has been projecting and what the results have been in terms of sales.

The image a product projects drives the product's brand identity. Image is defined as what the brand represents. This means that when a product's brand is being formed, the message or symbol you're trying to convey to a customer through the name, flavor, theme, etc. identifies the product. Use the following format to record your product(s) brand identity on the basis of product image.

Format 5

Product Image

	Image	
Product	**Brand Name**	**Brand Theme**
Model XY3	Fast Start	All in one
Model XY2	Fun House	So advanced it's simple

Appearance

Once you have established what your brand image will represent, you then must establish your product's appearance. Appearance is defined as the physical product itself and the package (if needed) that this product is sold in. Brand appearance is vital at the point of sale because how your product is perceived when sitting on a shelf can say: "Buy me."

Judgments of appearance can be based on substance, shape, color, size, labeling, or protective packaging. The key is getting the customer to act based on his or her perception of the product's appearance. Whether the perceived quality is real or imagined is not the issue—the customer's perception is the issue. You need to ask yourself the following questions regarding the brand appearance of your product:

- Does the package serve a useful purpose? Does it protect the product?
- Does the package communicate what your product/brand does or is?
- Does the product demonstrate a sellable and valuable attribute?

Use the following format to evaluate your brand appearance.

Format 6

Product Appearance

Product	Brand Name	Product Appearance	
		Actual (by itself)	Package (as sold)
Model XYZ	Fast Start	Black and silver, designed for a human hand	Clear plastic package with bold futuristic lettering
Model XY2	Fun House	Small and compact in stylish white case with bright electronic LCD lights	(product unseen) Protective whit carton with clearly marked instructions

Unit 2

Managing Your Product Line

Once your product line is established, you need to evaluate each product individually as well as your product line as a whole. First establish where each product falls in its life cycle. Then assess each product's sales growth rate, market share, and contributions to the company's total sales activity.

Like markets, all products have life cycles. Products pass through four stages: introduction, growth, maturity, and decline. Determining what stage your product currently is in can be a gray area. As a general rule, if you have a new product that is experiencing low sales you can consider that stage the introduction. Any sales increase that is sustained for a period of six or more months signals the growth stage of a product's life cycle. Once your sales begin to slow, but you do not notice a dramatic drop-off, the product is in maturity. As sales begin to drop at a rapid pace over a six-month period or sooner, the product is in decline.

It's not enough to establish what stage a product is in now, but you need to anticipate factors that might change the product's life cycle by lengthening or shortening a stage or moving the product from one stage to another.

Some product stages are long (5 to 10 years for automotive components) and some are short (18 months to 2 years for computer components); the key is to identify where your products are to see how much sales power they have left. To do this you must assess how long your products take to go through their individual life cycle stages as well as their overall life spans. Future product management and marketing strategies are based on the product's life cycle stage.

Use the following format to determine the life cycle stages of your product(s). Be sure to indicate the length of time that each product was in a certain stage. The examples shown should give you some guidance.

Format 7

Product Life Cycle Stage

19____

Product	Life Cycle Stage	Time	Factors
Model XYB	Maturity	2 years	New competition
Model XY2	Growth	1 year	Increased demand by customers

Establishing a product's life cycle stage in the product analysis affects the entire marketing process. An explanation of what marketing strategies should be used during each stage of the product life cycle may be found in Marketing Management, 6th edition, (Prentice-Hall, 1988).

PROFILING YOUR PRODUCT PORTFOLIO

Probably your most important activity is to establish your current product portfolio. Where your products are positioned in your product line mix can determine the direction of your subsequent product and marketing efforts. This will allow you to measure the products' levels of performance and to evaluate how they compare with one another in terms of sales volume. You can then determine if your product line needs any modifications, additions, or deletions.

It is important to link a product's growth and market share performance with its ability to contribute sales. You will perform this part of the exercise while establishing your product portfolio. Its purpose is to identify an actual sales volume percentage. This will allow you to cross-reference market share and growth rate with sales volume. Such an analysis will account for products that may be low sales volume-based performers but still have value such as serving to create awareness about the remainder of your product line.

Evaluating the Product Mix

The first exercise deals with using a perceptual map to demonstrate how your products rate as a group and individually. The portfolio model method used is based on your products' growth and market share. Both of these variables are driven by sales volume. The Boston Consulting

Group's Portfolio Analysis Matrix Model is the standard perceptual model that many marketers use to test portfolio validity. This model includes the following categories:

- Problem children—unpredictable, high-maintenance products

- Stars—low-risk, high-return products

- Dogs—high-risk, low-profit products

- Cash cows—mature, solid-return, low-maintenance products

Like product life cycle stages, your product portfolio model will help you identify what your products represent. Your goal is to assess how each product works with your other products from year to year and to determine each product's value in your product line.

Annual growth rate is set at 10 percent in the model; however, economic levels may require you to lower or raise standard growth rates to meet realistic expectations. For example, the standard growth rate for 1987 was 10 percent, but that for 1991 was 3 to 5 percent.

Market share is based on the competition's sales and the market potential. However, you not only need to note your relative market share, but what is acceptable for your industry.

The model and sample data are shown on Page 11. Each product is identified by a letter at the point where market share and growth rate intersect. Use this model to note a product's activity for the past three years and the next three years.

Determing Your Products' Sales Contribution

Another method of determining your products' value to your product line is to determine financial contribution. This is an excellent way to compare your products' performance; however, you must keep in mind each product's overall impact. For example, you may have a product that produces low sales volume with a low profit margin, but may lead a customer to purchase other products or may be recession-proof. These are product abilities that must be considered when evaluating a product's value.

The format on Page 12 will allow you to view each of your products' financial impact compared to your overall product line. First identify each product. Using your past sales reports, take each sales amount and divide it into the entire product lines sales. Your total percentages should equal 100 percent. In addition to each product's sales percentage, record your gross profit margin (in percentage) for each product.

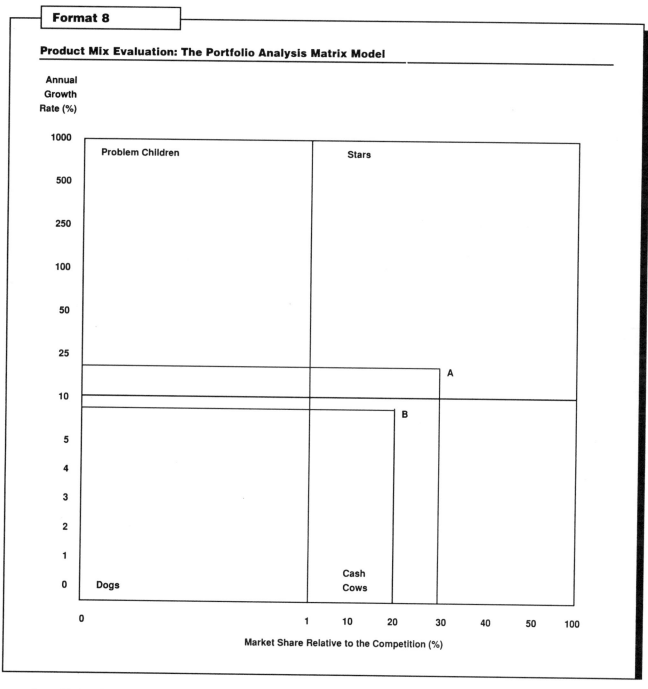

Format 8

Product Mix Evaluation: The Portfolio Analysis Matrix Model

Source: The Boston Consulting Group, Inc.

		Growth Rate	Market Share
Product: _Model XY3_	A	17%	30%
Product: _Model XY2_	B	8%	20%
Product: _____	C		
Product: _____	D		

Format 9

Product Sales Contribution

Product	Percentage of Sales	Gross Profit Margin
Model XY3	30%	43%
Model XY2	25%	50%
Total	100%	

Unit 3

Evaluating Product Sales Performance

Several effective methods may be used to measure product sales. You should always track your sales by product, customer type, geographic area, and store outlet, if applicable. Sales levels should be tracked by units and by dollar amounts, showing growth rates as well. If you have products that are new to the marketplace, sales will have to be predicted.

Historical Sales

Although it is valuable to look at sales records from as far back as possible, sales records from the past three years will give you the best indication of future sales. Use Formats 10–13 as shown. Growth rates are figured in units. Total growth rates are shown as an average.

Format 10

Sales by Product

Product(s)	19——			19——			19 ——		
	$	Units	%	$	Units	%	$	Units	%
Model XY3	$10,000	1,000	——	$11,000	1,500	50	$13,900	1,700	13
Model XY2	8,700	886	——	$10,500	1,000	13	12,000	1,200	20
Total									

Format 11

Sales by Customer Type

Product: _____ *XYZ* _____

Customer Type	19 ___			19 ___			19 ___		
	$	Units	%	$	Units	%	$	Units	%

Format 12

Sales by Geographic Area

Product: _____ *XYZ* _____

Geographic Area	19 ___			19 ___			19 ___		
	$	Units	%	$	Units	%	$	Units	%

Format 13

Sales by Store Outlet

Product: _____ *XYЗ* _____

Distribution Channel	19 ___ $	Units	%	19 ___ $	Units	%	19 ___ $	Units	%

Forecasted Product Sales

Formats 14 through 17 provide space for you to forecast your products' sales volume for the next three years by product, with breakdowns for each product by customer type, geographic area, and store outlet.

Format 14

Forecasted Sales by Product

Product	19 ___ $	Units	%	19 ___ $	Units	%	19 ___ $	Units	%
Total									

Format 15

Forecasted Sales by Customer Type

Product: _____ *XYZ* _____

Customer Type	19 ___			19 ___			19 ___		
	$	Units	%	$	Units	%	$	Units	%
Total									

Format 16

Forecasted Sales by Geographic Area

Product: _____ *XYZ* _____

Geographic Area	19 ___			19 ___			19 ___		
	$	Units	%	$	Units	%	$	Units	%
Total									

Format 17

Forecasted Sales by Store Outlet

Product: _____ *XYZ* _____   19 ___   19 ___   19 ___

Distribution Channel	$	Units	%	$	Units	%	$	Units	%
Total									

Estimating New Product Sales

If you have a new product that has just been put on the market, you'll have no historical sales data from which to forecast sales. You will need to estimate sales volume for a new product in other ways. Estimating is different than forecasting. Estimating means what you hope may happen, while forecasting means what you believe will happen. The difference is small but important in estimating a new product's sales performance.

The objectives of the following formats are to first determine what sales will be for your new products and, second, to examine the impact of these new products on current sales forecasts.

To obtain these data, use your own product research and historical sales performance of similar products. This information, along with current sales forecasts, will allow you to estimate sales of new products.

The formats allow you to predict your sales information based on four categories: product, customer type, geographic area, and store outlet.

Format 18

Estimated New Product Sales

Product	19___			19___			19___		
	$	Units	%	$	Units	%	$	Units	%
Total									

Format 19

Estimated New Product Sales by Customer Type

Product: _____*XYZ*_____

Customer Type	19___			19___			19___		
	$	Units	%	$	Units	%	$	Units	%
Total									

Format 20

Estimated New Product Sales by Geographic Area

Product: _____ *XYZ* _____

Geographic Area	19___			19___			19___		
	$	Units	%	$	Units	%	$	Units	%
Total									

Format 21

Estimated New Product Sales by Store Outlet

Product: _____ *XYZ* _____

Store Outlet	19___			19___			19___		
	$	Units	%	$	Units	%	$	Units	%
Total									

ANALYZING PRODUCT SALES PATTERNS

Sales performance in terms of raw sales volume is one way of assessing your performance levels. Another method is to analyze the sales performances as a whole and identify patterns, changes, and fluctuations. This helps you determine whether or not your sales run in cycles. This may allow you to forecast your sales better, as well as helping you plan production, inventory, and raw material purchases.

Identifying Sales Trends

The first objective is to identify whether or not your sales patterns reflect any continual change or trend. A trend is a consistent change in sales in any direction with any volume. If the trend holds for more than three years, then it may be considered a permanent pattern in your sales activity.

The format below provides you with a method of viewing how specific trends can have an impact on your product's sales, positively or negatively. First identify each product. Then list trend(s) that could affect your product. Then link that effect with its impact on your product. For example, let's say your product is designed to meet a specific customer of renting videotapes of movies. A trend that could affect that need would be development of a new technology such as video CDs or a new service such as pay-per-view cable TV.

Format 22

Product Sales Trends

Product	Trend	Impact
Model XY3	Use of CD technology	Must replace product soon
Model XY2	Customers wanting pay-per-view	Product losing value (sales), must change

Seasonal Fluctuations in Sales

Sales changes that are the same year after year are considered to be cyclical or seasonal. This means that for whatever reason, sales will move in the same direction with the same degree of impact each year. Your sales forecast can be adjusted to anticipate the seasonal changes.

Use the following format to track sales fluctuations by placing a point at the appropriate unit sales levels under each month, then connecting the points with a line. Remember, you will need to complete this chart for each of your products. Besides identifying product sales changes, this format allows you to overlay market sales for comparison purposes. Again, track the market sales by placing a point at the appropriate unit levels and then connecting the points to form a line.

The sample format here is based on unit sales of 1–10. Depending upon your sales volume you may need to adjust the scale to hundreds or even thousands of units.

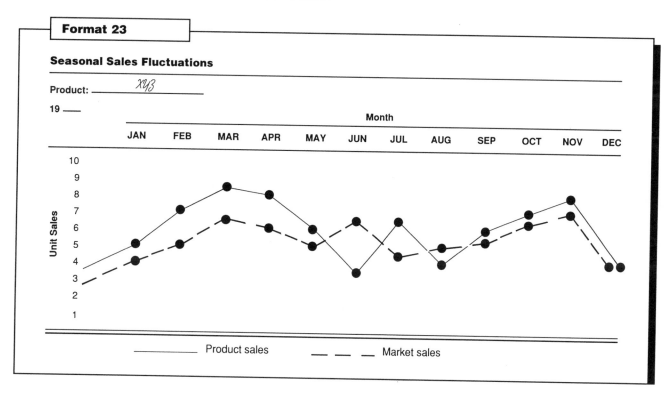

Unit 4

Determining Product Profitability

Of all the aspects of marketing management, profitability is number one. Sales are important, how you market is important, but determining how much money can be generated from a single product unit sale is crucial. As a marketer, it is important that you know your roles in your company's financial well-being. You should work very closely with your controller or accountant to ensure that your calculations are as accurate as possible.

ESTABLISHING YOUR PRODUCT PRICE/COST STRUCTURE

The first step in establishing the profitability of your product line is to develop your product price/cost structure. To do this, you must define your base price, special allowances such as volume discounts, and cost of goods sold. Then you will be able to establish your gross revenue, profit margin, and profit earning levels.

In determining your cost of goods sold, work with your accounting department to evaluate the cost formula to be used, which should include the following:

- Cost and sales volume relationships

- Extent of control over costs

In determining your pricing policies, again work with your accounting department to evaluate the price formula to be used, which should include the following:

- Impact of product management and distribution strategies

- Impact of costs, competition, and legal variables

- How much of an issue price is with your customers, and how it affects your overall marketing strategies

In addition, your accounting and finance departments, production, engineering, and legal counsel should participate in assessing current and future pricing practices.

The following format allows you to work through and establish your price/cost and profit structure. To use this format you must first identify each product. Next, establish the discount structure for the products. In this case, we will use volume discounting. Begin by counting the first unit (1) and then break down your discount structure in any increments. (The examples shown are in increments from 1–9, 10–19, and 20–50.) Finally, place your products' prices in the format.

The remainder of the format is filled out based on simple calculations. Subtract the dollar amount of each volume discount from your base price. (Remember that the first increment will have a discount of $0.) Then subtract the discount from the price base to find your revenue. Working with your accountant, you previously have established the cost of goods sold. Insert these numbers in the next line on the chart. Subtract your cost of goods sold from the revenue level to determine gross profit. Finally, convert the profit level into a percentage by taking the gross profit in dollars and dividing by the base price.

Format 24

Product Price/Cost Structure

Product: _____ *XY3* _____   Product: _____ *XY2* _____

Volume (units)	*(1–9)*	*(10–19)*	*(20–50)*		*(1 – +)*
Price ($)	*$689*	*$689*	*$689*		*$1,089*
Discount ($)	*00*	*50*	*100*		*00*
Revenue ($)	*689*	*639*	*589*		*1,089*
Cost of Goods Sold ($)	*260*	*260*	*260*		*520*
Gross Profit ($)	*$429*	*$379*	*$329*		*$569*
Gross Margin (%)	*62%*	*55%*	*48%*		*52%*

There are no general rules to determine if your profit margin is favorable. You will need to evaluate the final percentages based on industry standards and company goals. However, if your gross profit is very low—10% or less—you may want to reconsider the product's feasibility.

ANALYZING YOUR PRODUCT PROFIT STRUCTURE

After you have established your per-unit price/cost structure, your next objective is to produce your profit structure. You do this by combining the historical sales patterns for the last three years with your present price/cost structure to determine how much gross income can be produced. This information will reflect the strengths and weaknesses in your products' revenues and help you establish a product's value to the product line.

The next format allows you to combine your pricing structure with your past sales reports and your present sales forecasts to determine your

---

Format 25

Product Profit Structure

($ thousands)

Product: _____ *XYZ* _____

	19 __	19 __	19 __
Sales ($)	475,785	626,565	758,367
Sales (Units)	740	975	1,180
Growth (%)	N/A	32	21
Cost of Goods Sold ($)	209,300	303,160	404,042
Gross Profit ($)	266,485	323,405	354,325
Gross Margin (%)	56	52	47

---

revenue stream. Your source for sales volumes and growth rates is sales reporting and forecasting information. Your pricing structure will provide information on cost of goods sold, gross profit, and gross margins. Multiply your pricing data by your unit sales to determine your profit structure.

When you are analyzing your profit structure, you need to answer the following questions:

- Will customers accept a price that covers your cost of goods?

- Is growth of sales out-pacing increases in costs?

- Is there ample gross margin? (Depending on the industry standard, you need to have a strong gross margin to compensate for your net margins to be able to generate suitable profit levels. Work with your controller or accountant to determine an acceptable gross margin.)

- Are you making money?

- At what point in sales volume do you break even or do your total costs begin to drop off? What are the revenue implications of this break-even point? (Again, you will need to work with your financial department to perform a break-even analysis and to understand the total revenue picture. The break-even point will tell you when your sales start to represent true returns and how long it will take for the product to pay itself off.)

DETERMINING RETURN ON INVESTMENT (ROI)

The bottom line in marketing a product is making money. Although other factors do have value, and some products are more profitable than others, the amount of money a product can generate is what it is all about.

When a product is being considered for a market, the question is: "Is it worth the risk? How much money will I have to spend to make money?" Determining the return on investment (ROI) for a product is just that—

establishing the level of sales and profits it will take to, first, pay back the initial funding requirements, and second, provide an acceptable return on cash invested. In other words, ROI serves as a way to determine the value a product has for your business.

One method used to estimate ROI is the present value factor (PVF) system. The PVF tells you where your product is in its profit-making cycle and what you might expect when it fulfills its responsibility of paying back the initial investment.

To perform PVF you must first determine how much of an investment it is going to take to make a product viable in the marketplace. Then you need to establish the rate of return you would like. This is the amount of profit you want to receive as the result of investing your money. Although there are no standards, a 20–30% return is commonly considered to be fair. Next, you need to establish a timeframe for payback. How long a period of time is acceptable to you to receive return on your investment? Format 26 provides space for recording the pertinent data to answer these questions.

Investment Amount ($): _____

Desired Rate of Return (%): _____

Payback Timeframe (yrs): _____

Once these three pieces of data have been collected, you are ready to begin the process of determining payback and ROI using PVF. To do this you will need to use a PVF chart. (One is provided in this section of the book.) Working with your accountant or controller, determine your estimated after tax earnings (ATE). This information comes from your income statement and is driven by your pre-set sales forecast. Using the following format, place your ATE under each year in your payback timeframe. Next, use the PVF chart to match your desired rate of return with the PVF rate for each year in the timeframe. Multiply the ATE by the PVF for each year and use that number as the present value. Finally, total each year's present value to achieve a total value over the payback time frame. If the amount of total value exceeds your initial investment, the product should be marketed.

Format 26

Return on Investment (PVF)

Product: *XYZ*

Year	1	2	3	4	5	6	7	8	9	10	Total
After Tax Earnings ($)	50,000	50,500	60,000	60,750	70,000	70,000	60,000	40,000	20,000	8,000	489,250
Present Value Factor	.8264	.6830	.5645	.4665	.3855	.3186	.2633	.2176	.1799	.1486	
Present Value ($)	41,320	34,492	33,870	28,340	26,985	22,302	15,798	8,704	3,598	1,189	216,598

158, 379

The sample data used here were incorporated in the format to show how the PVF system works in determining ROI.

Investment Amount ($)	*100,000*
Desired Rate of Return (%)	*.21*
Payback Timeframe	*10 yrs.*
Present Value Total ($)	*216,598*
Actual Rate of Return (%)	*.53*

Present Value Factors

Future Year in which Dollar Is Received	Present Value of $1 When Yield or Discount Rate Is:												
	6%	9%	12%	15%	18%	21%	24%	27%	30%	35%	40%	45%	50%
1	.9434	.9174	.8929	.8696	.8475	.8264	.8065	.7874	.7692	.7407	.7143	.6897	.6667
2	.8900	.8417	.7972	.7561	.7182	.6830	.6504	.6200	.5917	.5487	.5102	.4756	.4444
3	.8396	.7722	.7118	.6575	.6086	.5645	.5245	.4882	.4552	.4064	.3644	.3280	.2963
4	.7921	.7084	.6355	.5718	.5158	.4665	.4230	.3844	.3501	.3011	.2603	.2262	.1975
5	.7473	.6499	.5674	.4972	.4371	.3855	.3411	.3027	.2693	.2230	.1859	.1560	.1317
6	.7050	.5963	.5066	.4323	.3704	.3186	.2751	.2383	.2072	.1652	.1328	.1076	.0878
7	.6651	.5470	.4523	.3759	.3139	.2633	.2218	.1877	.1594	.1224	.0949	.0742	.0585
8	.6274	.5019	.4039	.3269	.2660	.2176	.1789	.1478	.1226	.0906	.0678	.0512	.0390
9	.5919	.4604	.3606	.2843	.2255	.1799	.1443	.1164	.0943	.0671	.0484	.0353	.0260
10	.5584	.4224	.3220	.2472	.1911	.1486	.1164	.0916	.0725	.0497	.0346	.0243	.0173
11	.5268	.3875	.2875	.2149	.1619	.1228	.0938	.0721	.0558	.0368	.0247	.0168	.0116
12	.4970	.3555	.2567	.1869	.1372	.1015	.0757	.0568	.0429	.0273	.0176	.0116	.0077
13	.4688	.3262	.2292	.1625	.1163	.0839	.0610	.0447	.0330	.0202	.0126	.0080	.0051
14	.4423	.2992	.2046	.1413	.0985	.0693	.0492	.0352	.0254	.0150	.0090	.0055	.0034
15	.4173	.2745	.1827	.1229	.0835	.0573	.0397	.0277	.0195	.0111	.0064	.0038	.0023

Computations by Forrest G. Allen, 2/18/72.

Unit 5

Analyzing Your Production Capabilities

However great the demand for your products is, if you can't fill orders, your customers will be disappointed. You need to determine your ability to produce a product that fits your financial resources and can adjust to customer sales cycles. If yours is a service-based company, you need to address your ability to serve customers; in this environment, production takes on a different meaning, but the bottom line is to meet customer purchase demands.

ESTABLISHING YOUR PRODUCTION CAPACITY

The first step in determining your production capabilities is to establish your maximum production levels. It is important to determine what you consider comfortable production ranges, and when you need to enlarge your space, increase your machinery, add additional suppliers, and/or hire more workers. You then need to be prepared to adjust your cost structuring as required by these changes.

Format 27 provides a method of establishing your production activity levels. By determining how many workers it takes to produce your products, and what your various ranges of production speeds are, you can assess your ability to adjust and predict production strengths and weaknesses. These factors, combined with machinery and raw material supply, will help define what production capacity you can handle and support.

Use the chart on the bottom of Page 28 to record production information. You may want to reconfigure the format to accommodate your product line as a whole.

Your production capacity is one of the factors you will use in determining your sales forecasts; as a result, you need to plan what you believe to be realistic production levels.

Format 27

Production Capacity

Year	No. of Employees	Size of Facility	Production Volume Levels		
			Low	Medium	Maximum
19 —	22	Entire Plant (100 sq. ft.)	1,000	1,500	2,000
19 —	25	Entire Plant (100 sq. ft.)	1,200	1,700	2,200
19 —	25	Plant Expand (150 sq. ft.)	1,300	1,800	2,300

DETERMINING YOUR PRODUCTION RESOURCES AND LIMITATIONS

You need to determine the limits of your current production operations and at what point you will change them. Planned changes need to be compatible with future sales activities. You also need to indicate if any changes are anticipated in your internal or external resources. What impact will changes have on production? Changes which should be noted are new investments and changes in production-related costs.

Assessing Internal Operations

You need to establish the capacity of your internal production operations. This includes your manufacturing plant and production workers. You need to do this based on your present and future needs.

The chart below offers you a method of establishing your present needs and future plans. Use the three factors provided to identify your status.

Format 28A

Production Resources and Limitations

	Present Status	Future Plans
Production facilities	Small assembly area	New assembly area purchase for expansion (two years out)
Work force	Medium skilled	New education program to improve skill levels (next year)
Machinery	Old mechanical equipment	New computerized equipment (within the year)

Upon completion, this information will make you aware of your situation and what (if any) steps you may need to take to prepare for the future.

Assessing External Production Sources

You need to establish the capacity of your external production operations. This includes independent production subcontractors and their workers. You need to do this based on your present and future needs.

Format 28B

Production Resources and Limitations

	Present Status	Future Plans
Outside supplement		
Production facilities		

EVALUATING OPERATIONAL CONTROL

In this section, you are primarily concerned with events and actions that affect your production and delivery capabilities. You must identify present and alternative sources of supplies; and you must identify problem areas affecting product delivery and material availability as well as areas in which you have competitive advantages.

Use both of the following formats to define your delivery and supplier selections. By using the factors provided in the formats, you can better understand who is delivering your product to the customer and who is providing you with the material for manufacturing. This information will provide you with the basis for making decisions about these processes.

Product Delivery

The delivery of your product to your customers on time and undamaged is crucial. Delivery is the link between your production lines and fulfillment of the sales order. Whether you perform this task by internal or external means, you need to establish present and future sources of this capability.

Format 29A

Operational Control

Source	Present Status	Future Plans
In-House	*Using for 90% of all deliveries*	*No change*
Independent	*Using only for overflow*	*No change*

Materials Suppliers

The suppliers of the materials, parts, and components that comprise your product are also vital. You must establish relationships with suppliers who can provide quality materials when they are needed. Whether you depend on internal or external suppliers, you need to determine your present and future sources of materials.

You should also determine the importance of each supplier to your operations, considering lead time requirements, risk of shortages, and terms of contracts.

Format 29B

Operational Control

Source	Present Status	Future Plans
In-House	*Have exclusive contracts*	*Will branch out to have alternatives*
Independent	*Used only when needed*	*Will open up for bids*

Assessing Competitive Operating Advantages

You should make a summary analysis of competitive advantages in your overall operational control. These competitive advantages will include production capacity, delivery of product, and suppliers' ability to meet your needs. Advantages to identify include proprietary techniques, level of experience, and lower costs. These strengths can later translate into marketing strategies.

Unit 6

Assessing Your Legal Situation

Yes, in marketing, your legal situation needs to be addressed. You need to first make sure that your marketing activity is legal. You must not undertake any activity that is in violation of current or pending laws. Your objective, as a marketer, is to identify legal issues that may be confronting your product's entry into the marketplace. You must protect yourself from lawsuits by someone who may claim you have stolen ideas and also prevent anyone from stealing your ideas so you will not have to take legal action against them.

EVALUATING PROTECTION OF COPYRIGHTS, PATENTS, TRADE SECRETS, AND TRADEMARKS

You must make sure you have applied for the appropriate legal protection for your products. Although some products can't be protected, most can be to some degree; it is important to make sure these products are covered. Also, any legally required labeling must be used.

The format below allows you to record the status of any legal efforts that are being undertaken on behalf of your product(s). The sample pertains to the status of patent filing procedures for two different models of a product.

Format 30

Copyrights, Patents, Trade Secrets, and Trademarks

Product	Filing Status	Date Fully Covered
Model XYZ	Phase 1 Filing (patent pending)	Next year – June 1
Model XY2	Not patentable	Not available

ASSESSING PRODUCT LIABILITY

You need to measure what your degree of exposure is to product liability. In this day of personal injury litigation, you need to determine if your product could hurt the user or anyone nearby. If you are liable for damages caused by your product, then you have to determine your level of risk and most probably obtain liability insurance. If insurance is obtained, its cost needs to be integrated into your general expenses.

The format below offers you a method of evaluating the amount of liability exposure you may or may not have. The purpose of this exercise is to help you determine the likelihood that your product could create an unfair and/or unsafe situation due to negligence in its creation, design, or use. This determination should come from your attorney. You then need to discuss the steps you would take to protect yourself from the legal consequences of this negligence. This could involve product liability insurance, labeling awareness, liability releases, legal positioning, or *nothing*. Doing nothing is not as bad as it sounds. You must meet the rules governing your product's existence and it must perform fairly and safely, within reason. However, many times companies feel that it is cheaper to fight and/or settle law suits than to take on the cost of preventing problems from arising.

Format 31

Product Liability

Product	Level of Exposure	Cost of Insurance
Model XYЗ	Very small	No insurance
Model XY2	Medium to high	Heavy insurance $1,000.000 coverage $20,000 cost per year

Product liability costs are key, and it is marketing's role to provide this information to the accountant or controller who is figuring the product's financials.

EXAMINING OUTSTANDING CONTRACTS AND AGREEMENTS

Another legal factor is outstanding contracts with vendors, suppliers, distributors, salespeople, competitors, and current and former employees. Contracts are designed to protect individuals' rights; you need to make sure that any marketing activity you undertake is not in violation of these contracts.

The format below provides a method of recording your marketing legal situation. For each product, determine what, if any, legal issues are pending. This analysis will help you to determine if you need outside funding or if there is a legal problem that could delay or halt a product's manufacturing.

Format 32

Legal Agreements

Product	Non-Disclosure Agreements	Non-Compete Agreements	Outstanding/Pending Product Litigation
Model XYZ	*None*	*One—with former joint venture partner*	*None*
Model XY2	*None*	*None*	*Yes—Former stock owner, for compensation*

Unit 7

Evaluating Product Research and Development

Someone once said regarding football fans, "The offense puts fans in the seats, the defense keeps them there." The same thing holds true in marketing: your current products produce sales and revenue, your research and development activities maintain them. In other words, no product, even with enhancements and updates, lasts forever. As a result, you must constantly look for new products.

ASSESSING PAST PRODUCT DEVELOPMENT

The first thing you need to examine is former products. The objective is to identify the status of products you have or have not added to your product line. Format 33 provides space in which to list products under development. Be sure to list the date a product was released into the market (if any) and a performance rating.

Format 33

Products under Development

Product	Purpose	Target Market	Results
Model 123 Cleaner	Home cleaner	Women 30–40 yrs.	Released 6-30-90. Very successful.
Model 321 Cleaner	Auto cleaner	Men 20–30 yrs.	Terminated—did not test well with market.

You may want to expand the results section of this format to include information such as the product's performance at the target market and prototype stages.

EVALUATING PRODUCT DEVELOPMENT STATUS

Once you have established what you have done in the past, you then need to determine the status of present product developments. Your objective is to determine where specific products are in the research and development stages. Possible status points include:

- Concept Stage—idea generation

- Market Analysis Stage—earning potential

- Product Testing Stage—prototype

- Product Trial Stage—controlled field usage

- Product Launch Stage—full production/release

A product is in constant motion. As you complete the exercise below, your objective is to bring definition to a product's status and activity at that stage. In determining the status of new products, remember to include not only products that exist in your own environment but also those products you are acquiring through acquisition, merger, joint venture, and/or licensing arrangements with another party. The objective is to identify where you stand with products that may or may not be added to your existing product line.

Format 34

Product Development Status

Product Description	Stage	Purpose/Use	Target Market	Expected Release Date
Model 101	Concept	Home Cleaning	Hispanic Women	2–93
Model XXX	Product Testing	Home Repair	White Men	1–94

ESTABLISHING PRODUCT TESTING AND RESEARCH ACTIVITIES

Once you have determined past and present product development activities, you need to evaluate the research and testing procedures you are using. We will first define a few terms that will help you with your evaluation.

- **Product Research**—A form of research conducted directly with the customer at various stages of the product's development. The purpose is to determine the customer's perception of the product, what needs the product must fill for the customer to purchase it, and how to make the customer a loyal customer.

- **Performance Testing**—An actual physical test in which a product's features are evaluated, usually in a controlled, scientific setting. Testing can be conducted strictly as a function of the marketing department or as a combined effort between marketing research staffs and manufacturing/production.

- **Market Research**—The process of identifying the areas into which a product will be sold. These areas (markets) are evaluated on criteria such as competition, size, legal regulations, and overall consumer purchasing patterns.

- **Marketing Research**—An umbrella term used to describe all research acts that fall under the business functions of marketing. More specifically, *marketing research* is used to define an ongoing research application (such as customer satisfaction) that is usually evaluated as part of an annual marketing plan.

Your objective in this section is to establish what types of research or testing activities are being used and what you hope to verify or determine about your product(s).

The next format provides a method of establishing what testing and research activities are currently underway. This allows you to view the various forms of testing in manufacturing and marketing environments and evaluate results.

Format 35

Product Testing

Product	Stage	Activities Conducted	Results
Model 990	Product Testing	Product Research/Field Customer Acceptance	Modifications to Target Markets
Model 133	Product Trials	Product Research/Customer Brand Awareness	Packaging Changes

The New Product Development Process

The key to product research in the new product development process is to work with your R & D and production departments in the overseeing of the product's development. Clear communication between all departments is crucial. Exhibit 7–1 diagrams the phases in the product research process.

EXHIBIT 7–1
The Product Research Process

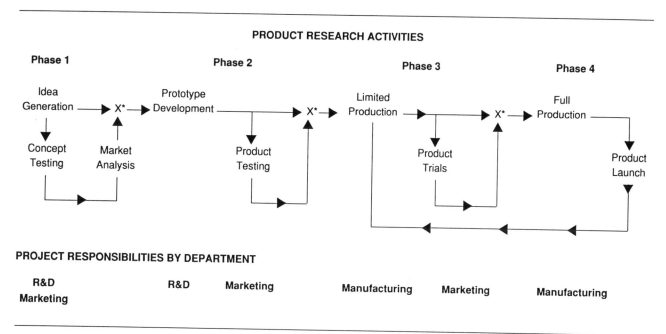

PRODUCT RESEARCH ACTIVITIES

PROJECT RESPONSIBILITIES BY DEPARTMENT

* An "X" indicates points at which a product evaluation should be undertaken to check product viability.

Phase 1: Testing Product Viability

In idea generation, you have identified a need, problem, or opportunity that needs to be satisfied by a product. You envision a product idea and determine if the idea has merit.

Concept testing takes the idea and turns it into a working model. You are refining the idea by screening and making initial calculations. Another consideration is whether or not the concept meets the guidelines of current marketing objectives, strategies, and resources.

You need to create a scoring model to use internally in evaluating a product's potential value. The format shown in Figure 7–2 could be used.

FIGURE 7–2
A Product Scoring Model

(A) Measurement Factor	(B) Relative Weight	(C) Factor Ranking	Score (B × C =)
Product Attractiveness			
1. Meets customer needs or desires	.10	8	.80
2. Life cycle length	.03	6	.18
3. Portfolio enhancement	.06	7	.42
4. Sales contributor	.05	7	.35
5. Financial performer	.09	10	.90
6. Production time	.04	9	.36
7. Product liability	.07	5	.35
8. Future Enhancements	.01	6	.06
9. Required operations changes	.02	10	.20
10. Market potential	.08	9	.72
Total			4.34

In this scoring model, the relative weight adjusts for the importance of the measurement factor. Factors are ranked on a scale of 1 through 10, with 10 being the best. The more positive the impact of the factor the higher the ranking. The factor's relative weight is multiplied by its ranking to produce a score for the factor. Scores are interpreted as follows:

Score	Product Rating
4.50 +	Super star product
3.50 – 4.49	Strong product
2.50 – 3.49	Average product
2.49 –	Weak product

Once you have defined your product concept, you must conduct a market analysis to determine if it is a profitable project. You need to establish the marketing demand, risks, rewards, legal issues, competition, financial resources needed, limitations and impact in the market, and how the concept relates to your existing product line. If the product can meet market requirements, then legal protection and commercialization control should be taken care of.

Phase 2: Testing the Product Prototype

At this point, you have decided to move forward with this new product concept. Now you are ready to create a product prototype and present it to the customers who may desire it. Your objective is to qualify customers' perceptions and preferences toward your product relative to the marketplace. This stage is primarily concerned with customer acceptance, and the following sample questions should be asked:

Will customer recognize the product's value?

Will they seek the product out?

How often will they purchase the product?

How much will they pay for the product?

What do they like and dislike about the product, and how would they change it?

You need to evaluate not only the product itself, but also its brand identity, the attractiveness of its packaging, and its value-added services such as warranties and installation.

Phase 3: Product Trials

After you have made the changes, enhancements, and refinements to the product indicated by the prototype testing to make a marketable, functional product, the next step is to evaluate the product in the real world. You do this by producing and distributing a limited amount of the product and targeting it at selected customers at test sites. This testing is the final safety guard before the product is marketed widely.

Phase 4: Product Launch and Marketing Research

Assuming you will market this product yourself rather than sell the license rights to someone else, the next step is marketing the product and then assessing the level of customer satisfaction after the sale. You do this by measuring the reactions of a selected group of customers in areas such as perception of product quality, degree of loyalty to the product, and whether product expectations were met. The feedback you receive can once again turn into product improvements and innovations for this product and other product ideas.

Note: *There has been a lot of talk lately about speeding up the product development process. There is no doubt that many companies have slowed this process to the point where it is very ineffective, and there is nothing wrong with accelerating the process. However, it is very important to make sure that each phase of research is conducted, that the data obtained are timely and accurate and are used appropriately in the process, and that each phase is performed in the proper order.*

Format 36

Product Research

Product	Type of Research Performed	Results Obtained
Model XY3	Product Testing	Package is too bulky, product recognition is good.
Model XY2	Product Trials	New package good.

Part 2

Data Reporting: Formats

After you have input and processed the product data, the next step is to place that information in a format suitable for presentation. There is no need to include these exact formats in your final document; instead, a solid product analysis blends written narrative segments with matrix models and charts containing hard data. This breaks up the data being presented and gives the reader a sense of a beginning and an end.

Formats for Unit 1

Identifying Your Products

Formats 1–6 should be used to help you identify the characteristics of your products. See Unit 1 in Part 1 for explanations and examples of the formats.

Format 1

Product Purpose

Past Products (Have been discontinued over the last three years. Ranked by order of product/market introduction date.)

Product	Purpose

Format 1 (Continued)

Product Purpose

Present Products (Existing products for sale for the next three years. Ranked by order of product/market introduction date.)

Product	Purpose

Format 2

Target Market

Past Products (Have been discontinued over the last three years. Ranked by order of product/market introduction date.)

Product   **Customer/Target Market(s)**

Format 2 (Continued)

Target Market

Present Products (Existing products for sale for the next three years. Ranked by order of product/market introduction date.)

Product   **Customer/Target Market(s)**

Format 3

Distinctive Product Factors

Past Products (Have been discontinued over the last three years. Ranked in order of importance.)

Product	Distinctive Factors

Format 3 (Continued)

Distinctive Product Factors

Present Products (Existing products for sale for the next three years. Ranked in order of importance.)

Product   **Distinctive Factors**

Format 4

Product Features and Benefits

Past Products

Product	Features	Benefits

Format 4 (Continued)

Product Features and Benefits

Present Products

Product	Features	Benefits

Format 5

Product Image

Past Products

Product	Image	
	Brand Name	**Brand Theme**

Format 5 (Continued)

Product Image

Present Products

Product	Image	
	Brand Name	Brand Theme

Format 6

Product Appearance

Past Products

Product	Brand Name	Product Appearance	
		Actual (by itself)	Package (as sold)

Format 6 (Continued)

Product Appearance

Present Products

Product	Brand Name	Product Appearance	
		Actual (by itself)	Package (as sold)

Managing Your Product Line

Formats 7–9 should be used to help you identify the characteristics of your products. See Unit 2 in Part 1 for explanations and examples of the formats.

Format 7

Product Life Cycle Stage

Last Three Years

19 _____

Product	Life Cycle Stage	Time	Factors

19 _____

Product	Life Cycle Stage	Time	Factors

19 _____

Product	Life Cycle Stage	Time	Factors

Format 7 (Continued)

Product Life Cycle Stage

Next Three Years

19 ____

Product	Life Cycle Stage	Time	Factors

19 ____

Product	Life Cycle Stage	Time	Factors

19 ____

Product	Life Cycle Stage	Time	Factors

Format 8

Product Mix Evaluation: The Portfolio Analysis Matrix Model

Last Three Years

19 ____

Annual Growth Rate (%)

1000	Problem Children	Stars
500		
250		
100		
50		
25		
10		
5		
4		
3		
2		
1		Cash Cows
0	Dogs	

0   1   10   20   30   40   50   100

Market Share Relative to the Competition (%)

Source: The Boston Consulting Group, Inc.

Format 8 (Continued)

Product Mix Evaluation: The Portfolio Analysis Matrix Model

Last Three Years

19 _____

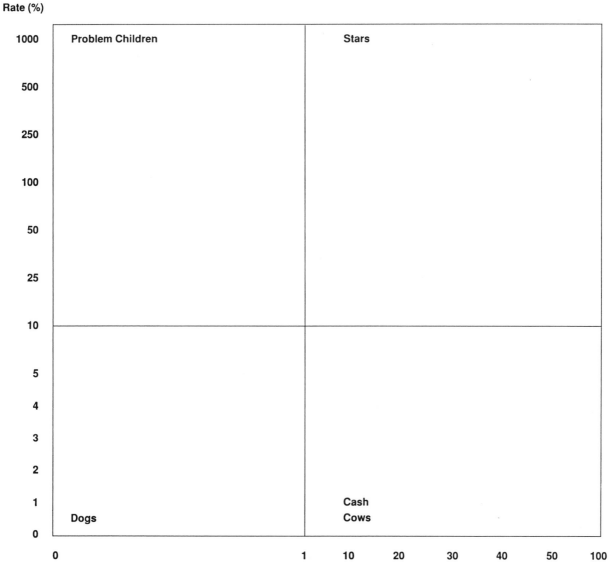

Annual Growth Rate (%)

- Problem Children
- Stars
- Dogs
- Cash Cows

1000 · 500 · 250 · 100 · 50 · 25 · 10 · 5 · 4 · 3 · 2 · 1 · 0

0 · 1 · 10 · 20 · 30 · 40 · 50 · 100

Market Share Relative to the Competition (%)

Source: The Boston Consulting Group, Inc.

Format 8 (Continued)

Product Mix Evaluation: The Portfolio Analysis Matrix Model

Last Three Years

19 _____

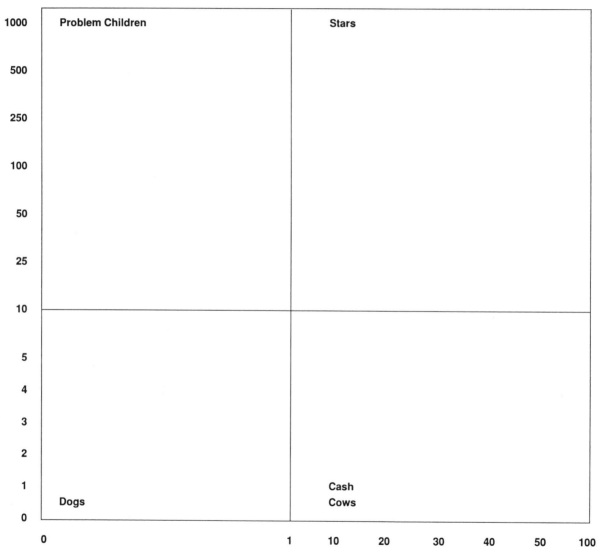

Annual
Growth
Rate (%)

Problem Children

Stars

1000

500

250

100

50

25

10

5

4

3

2

1

0

Dogs

Cash
Cows

0   1   10   20   30   40   50   100

Market Share Relative to the Competition (%)

Format 8 (Continued)

Product Mix Evaluation: The Portfolio Analysis Matrix Model

Last Three Years

19 ___

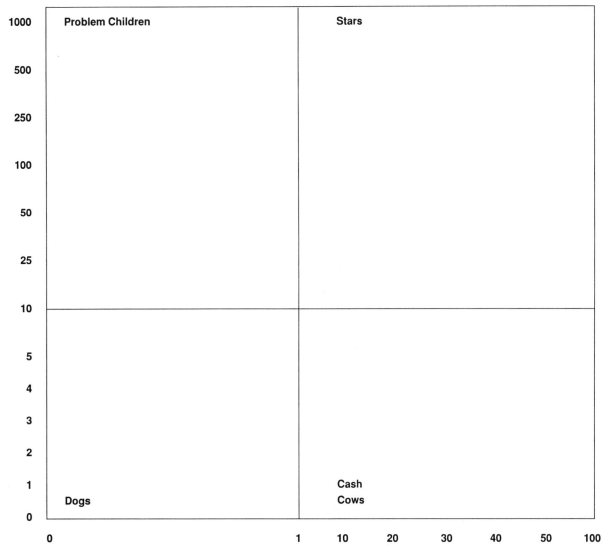

Source: The Boston Consulting Group, Inc.

Format 8 (Continued)

Product Mix Evaluation: The Portfolio Analysis Matrix Model

Last Three Years

19 _____

Annual
Growth
Rate (%)

	Problem Children		Stars	

1000

500

250

100

50

25

10

5

4

3

2

1

Dogs

Cash
Cows

0

0   1   10   20   30   40   50   100

Market Share Relative to the Competition (%)

Source: The Boston Consulting Group, Inc.

Format 8 (Continued)

Product Mix Evaluation: The Portfolio Analysis Matrix Model

Last Three Years

19 ___

**Annual
Growth
Rate (%)**

	Problem Children	Stars
1000		
500		
250		
100		
50		
25		
10		
5		
4		
3		
2		
1		Cash Cows
0	Dogs	

0   1   10   20   30   40   50   100

Market Share Relative to the Competition (%)

Source: The Boston Consulting Group, Inc.

Format 9

Product Sales Contribution

Last Three Years

19 ____

Product	Percentage of Sales	Gross Profit Margin
Total	**100%**	

19 ____

Product	Percentage of Sales	Gross Profit Margin
Total	**100%**	

19 ____

Product	Percentage of Sales	Gross Profit Margin
Total	**100%**	

Format 9 (Continued)

Product Sales Contribution

Next Three Years

19 ___

Product	Percentage of Sales	Gross Profit Margin
Total	**100%**	

19 ___

Product	Percentage of Sales	Gross Profit Margin
Total	**100%**	

19 ___

Product	Percentage of Sales	Gross Profit Margin
Total	**100%**	

Evaluating Product Sales Performance

Formats 10–23 should be used to help you identify the characteristics of your products. See Unit 3 in Part 1 for explanations and examples of the formats.

Format 10

Sales by Product

Product(s)	19 ___			19 ___			19 ___		
	$	Units	%	$	Units	%	$	Units	%
Total									

Format 11

Sales by Customer Type

($ thousands)

Product: _____

Customer Type	19___			19___			19___		
	$	Units	%	$	Units	%	$	Units	%
Total									

Product: _____

Customer Type	19___			19___			19___		
	$	Units	%	$	Units	%	$	Units	%
Total									

Format 12

Sales by Geographic Area

($ thousands)

Product: _____	19___			19___			19___		
Geographic Area	$	Units	%	$	Units	%	$	Units	%
Total									

Product: _____	19___			19___			19___		
Geographic Area	$	Units	%	$	Units	%	$	Units	%
Total									

Format 13

Sales by Store Outlet

($ thousands)

Product: _____	19 ___			19 ___			19 ___		
Store Outlet	$	Units	%	$	Units	%	$	Units	%
Total									

Product: _____	19 ___			19 ___			19 ___		
Store Outlet	$	Units	%	$	Units	%	$	Units	%
Total									

70

Format 14

Forecasted Sales by Product

($ thousands)	19___			19___			19___		
Product(s)	$	Units	%	$	Units	%	$	Units	%
Total									

Format 15

Forecasted Sales by Customer Type

($ thousands)

Product: _____ 19 ___ 19 ___ 19 ___

Customer Type	$	Units	%	$	Units	%	$	Units	%
Total									

Product: _____ 19 ___ 19 ___ 19 ___

Customer Type	$	Units	%	$	Units	%	$	Units	%
Total									

Format 16

Forecasted Sales by Geographic Area

($ thousands)

Product: _____

Geographic Area	19___			19___			19___		
	$	Units	%	$	Units	%	$	Units	%
Total									

Product: _____

Geographic Area	19___			19___			19___		
	$	Units	%	$	Units	%	$	Units	%
Total									

Format 17

Forecasted Sales by Store Outlet

($ thousands)

Product: _____	19 ___			19 ___			19 ___		
Distribution Channel	$	Units	%	$	Units	%	$	Units	%
Total									

Product: _____	19 ___			19 ___			19 ___		
Store Outlet	$	Units	%	$	Units	%	$	Units	%
Total									

Format 18

Estimated New Product Sales

($ thousands)	19___			19___			19___		
Product(s)	$	Units	%	$	Units	%	$	Units	%
Total									

Format 19

Estimated New Product Sales by Customer Type

($ thousands)

Product: _____   19 ___   19 ___   19 ___

Customer Type	$	Units	%	$	Units	%	$	Units	%
Total									

Product: _____   19 ___   19 ___   19 ___

Customer Type	$	Units	%	$	Units	%	$	Units	%
Total									

Format 20

Estimated New Product Sales by Geographic Area

($ thousands)

Product: _____	19 __			19 __			19 __		
Geographic Area	$	Units	%	$	Units	%	$	Units	%
Total									

Product: _____	19 __			19 __			19 __		
Geographic Area	$	Units	%	$	Units	%	$	Units	%
Total									

Format 21

Estimated New Product Sales by Store Outlet

($ thousands)

Product: _____   19 ____   19 ____   19 ____

Store Outlet	$	Units	%	$	Units	%	$	Units	%
Total									

Product: _____   19 ____   19 ____   19 ____

Store Outlet	$	Units	%	$	Units	%	$	Units	%
Total									

Format 22

Product Sales Trends

Last Three Years

Product	Trend	Impact

Format 22 (Continued)

Product Sales Trends

Next Three Years

Product	Trend	Impact

Format 23

Seasonal Sales Fluctuations

Last Three Years

Product: ——————————————

19 __						Month						
	JAN	FEB	MAR	APR	MAY	JUN	JUL	AUG	SEP	OCT	NOV	DEC

Unit Sales

```
10
 9
 8
 7
 6
 5
 4
 3
 2
 1
```

19 __						Month						
	JAN	FEB	MAR	APR	MAY	JUN	JUL	AUG	SEP	OCT	NOV	DEC

Unit Sales

```
10
 9
 8
 7
 6
 5
 4
 3
 2
 1
```

19 __						Month						
	JAN	FEB	MAR	APR	MAY	JUN	JUL	AUG	SEP	OCT	NOV	DEC

Unit Sales

```
10
 9
 8
 7
 6
 5
 4
 3
 2
 1
```

Format 23 (Continued)

Seasonal Sales Fluctuations

Next Three Years

Product: _____

19 ___

						Month						
Unit Sales	JAN	FEB	MAR	APR	MAY	JUN	JUL	AUG	SEP	OCT	NOV	DEC
10												
9												
8												
7												
6												
5												
4												
3												
2												
1												

19 ___

						Month						
Unit Sales	JAN	FEB	MAR	APR	MAY	JUN	JUL	AUG	SEP	OCT	NOV	DEC
10												
9												
8												
7												
6												
5												
4												
3												
2												
1												

19 ___

						Month						
Unit Sales	JAN	FEB	MAR	APR	MAY	JUN	JUL	AUG	SEP	OCT	NOV	DEC
10												
9												
8												
7												
6												
5												
4												
3												
2												
1												

Determining Product Profitability

Formats 24–26 should be used to help you identify the characteristics of your products. See Unit 4 in Part 1 for explanations and examples of the formats.

Format 24

Product Price/Cost Structure

Last Three Years

19 ___

Product: _____   Product: _____

Volume (units)

Price ($)

Discount ($)

Revenue ($)

Cost of Goods Sold ($)

Gross Profit ($)

Gross Margin (%)

19 ___

Product: _____

Volume (units)

Price ($)

Discount ($)

Revenue ($)

Cost of Goods Sold ($)

Gross Profit ($)

Gross Margin (%)

19 ___

Product: _____

Volume (units)

Price ($)

Discount ($)

Revenue ($)

Cost of Goods Sold ($)

Gross Profit ($)

Gross Margin (%)

Format 24 (Continued)

Product Price/Cost Structure

Next Three Years

19 ___

Product: _____   Product: _____

Volume (units)

Price ($)

Discount ($)

Revenue ($)

Cost of Goods Sold ($)

Gross Profit ($)

Gross Margin (%)

19 ___

Product: _____

Volume (units)

Price ($)

Discount ($)

Revenue ($)

Cost of Goods Sold ($)

Gross Profit ($)

Gross Margin (%)

19 ___

Product: _____

Volume (units)

Price ($)

Discount ($)

Revenue ($)

Cost of Goods Sold ($)

Gross Profit ($)

Gross Margin (%)

Format 25

Product Profit Structure

Last Three Years ($ thousands)

Product: _____	19 ___	19 ___	19 ___
Sales ($)			
Sales (Units)			
Discount ($)			
Growth (%)			
Cost of Goods Sold ($)			
Gross Profit ($)			
Gross Margin (%)			

Total Product Line

Sales ($)			
Sales (Units)			
Growth (%)			
Cost ($)			
Gross Profit ($)			
Gross Margin (%)			

Format 25 (Continued)

Product Profit Structure

Next Three Years ($ thousands)

Product: _____	19 ___	19 ___	19 ___
Sales ($)			
Sales (Units)			
Discount ($)			
Growth (%)			
Cost of Goods Sold ($)			
Gross Profit ($)			
Gross Margin (%)			

Total Product Line

Sales ($)			
Sales (Units)			
Growth (%)			
Cost ($)			
Gross Profit ($)			
Gross Margin (%)			

Format 26

Return on Investment (PVF)

Product:

Year	1	2	3	4	5	6	7	8	9	10	Total
After Tax Earnings ($)											
Present Value Factor											
Present Value ($)											

Product:

Year	1	2	3	4	5	6	7	8	9	10	Total
After Tax Earnings ($)											
Present Value Factor											
Present Value ($)											

Product:

Year	1	2	3	4	5	6	7	8	9	10	Total
After Tax Earnings ($)											
Present Value Factor											
Present Value ($)											

Product:

Year	1	2	3	4	5	6	7	8	9	10	Total
After Tax Earnings ($)											
Present Value Factor											
Present Value ($)											

Analyzing Your Production Capabilities

Formats 27–29 should be used to help you analyze your current and future production capabilities. See Unit 5 in Part 1 for explanations and examples of the formats.

Format 27

Production Capacity

Last Three Years

Year	No. of Employees	Size of Facility	Production Volume Levels		
			Low	Medium	Maximum
19 ___					
19 ___					
19 ___					

Next Three Years

Year	No. of Employees	Size of Facility	Production Volume Levels		
			Low	Medium	Maximum
19 ___					
19 ___					
19 ___					

Format 28

Production Resources and Limitations: Internal Operations

	Present Status	Future Plans
Production facilities		
Work force		
Machinery		

Production Resources and Limitations: External Production Sources

	Present Status	Future Plans
Outside Supplement		
Production facilities		

Format 29

Operational Control

Delivery

Source	Present Status	Future Plans
In-House		
Independent		

Suppliers

Source	Present Status	Future Plans
In-House		
Independent		

Competitive Operating Advantages:

Assessing Your Legal Situation

Formats 30–32 should be used to help you examine legal issues related to your products. See Unit 6 in Part 1 for explanations and examples of the formats.

Format 30

Copyrights, Patents, Trade Secrets, and Trademarks

Product	Filing Status	Date Fully Covered

Format 31

Product Liability

Product	Level of Exposure	Cost of Insurance

Format 32

Legal Agreements

Product	Non-Disclosure Agreements	Non-Compete Agreements	Outstanding/Pending Product Litigation

Evaluating Product Research and Development

Formats 33–36 should be used to help you evaluate your product research and development. See Unit 7 in Part 1 for explanations and examples of the formats.

Format 33

Products under Development

Past Products

Product	Purpose	Target Market	Results

Present Products

Product	Purpose	Target Market	Results

Format 34

Product Development Status

Past Products

Product Description	Stage	Purpose/Use	Target Market	Expected Release Date

Present Products

Product Description	Stage	Purpose/Use	Target Market	Expected Release Date

Format 35

Product Testing

Past Products

Product	Stage	Activities Conducted	Results

Present Products

Product	Stage	Activities Conducted	Expected Results

Format 36

Product Research

Past Products

Product	Type of Research Performed	Results Obtained

Present Products

Product	Type of Research	Expected Results

About the Author

David Parmerlee is a marketing analyst and planner who works with selected clients. He is past Vice President of the Marketing Management Services Group at American Marketmetrics, Inc. A marketer with more than 12 years of experience, his approach has a financial orientation rather than the more traditional communications approach. His background is in secondary and audit research with a focus on process-based planning and implementation.

Parmerlee has worked for several major corporations, including Anheuser-Busch, Pitney Bowes, and Arthur Young (now Ernst & Young). He has represented clients in industrial, consumer, and service-based markets and has written articles for regional and national publications. He is a member of the Direct Marketing Association and the American Mar-keting Association, where he serves on the board of directors and the national board of standards for professional development and certification.

Parmerlee received his degrees in marketing and advertising from Ball State University in Muncie, Indiana. He is also certified as a consultant specializing in training and ethics.